Workbook and Supplemental Guide

Applying the Principles Found in
The Welfare of My Neighbor

by Amy L. Sherman
Director of Urban Ministries, Trinity Presbyterian Church
Adjunct Fellow, Manhattan Institute

Deanna Carlson, Editor
Director of Community Outreach, Family Research Council

Workbook and Supplemental Guide: Applying the Principles Found in *The Welfare of My Neighbor*

Published by Family Research Council
801 G Street, NW, Washington, DC 20001
All rights reserved.

Printed in the United States of America.

ISBN 1-55872-003-0

Unless otherwise noted, Bible quotations are from the New International Version.

This workbook and supplemental guide is a revision and expansion of *Establishing a Welfare-to-Work Mentoring Ministry: A Practical "How-To" Manual*, published by The Center for Civic Innovation at The Manhattan Institute (New York, 1998). The material in Chapters 1, 2 and 5 and Appendices B and D are published with permission by the Center for Public Justice. They were originally distributed at a 1998 Center for Public Justice conference called "Working Together to Serve the Needy: Welfare Reform and the Faith Communities in Greater Philadelphia." Family Research Council expresses deepest thanks to The Manhattan Institute and The Center for Public Justice for permission to reprint this material.

This workbook and supplemental guide is for *The Welfare of My Neighbor: Living Out Christ's Love for the Poor* by Deanna Carlson (Washington, D.C.: Family Research Council, 1999).

Cover Image: © Slocum-Quinn. "The Banquet," 1997. Used by permission.
The painting depicts Monday lunch at the "Southeast White House" in Washington, D.C. Also affectionately known as "the Little White House," this Christ-centered ministry house sits on Pennsylvania Ave., SE (in a low-income neighborhood called Anacostia). There, relationships are started between Washington's powerful and powerless for the greater good of children and families in need in Washington, D.C.

Table of Contents

Foreword

By Deanna Carlson

Having been born and reared in the fellowship of a Christian congregation, I have been involved with various church-based ministries, both as a giver and a receiver. The most gratifying ministries I have participated in have been based on relationships. One such ministry, where I was the receiver, continues to change my life.

Called the "core group," this was a church-based mentoring ministry with a simple goal: for a group of girls to meet regularly with a Christian leader. I committed to the "core group" in seventh grade because I needed friends, having moved to a new church. I was joined with twelve other girls (all equally feisty and willful), and we were put under the love and care of a volunteer leader, Diana. None of us had any experience with this type of ministry, nor did we make things easy for Diana.

However, one thing stood out through all our successes and failures together. We were committed to one another. What started out as one young leader's commitment to us has evolved into a lifetime commitment of Christ-centered friendship. I have now been in this "core group" of 12 "girls" for over 20 years. My relationship with the other girls and our leader (who is now a peer) has easily been one of the most transformational aspects of my Christian walk.

I am a believer in relational ministries because my life has been forever changed by Christians investing in me with not just their pocketbooks, but their very souls. I can't even imagine what would have happened to me if my church had decided I needed simply "things" such as money or a roof over my head, and had failed to steer me towards heart-to-heart, Christian relationships.

I believe that what is missing from many of our church-based outreach ministries is relationships. I continue to be inspired by new ministries to those *inside* the church that are rooted in the Bible and *people*, such as adult fellowship groups, youth groups, and new moms groups. On the other hand, I am dismayed that many of our ministries to those *outside* the church are based on the Bible and *things*. These include ministries that provide for legitimate physical needs, such as clothes closets, food pantries or temporary housing, but are not built on a foundation of relationships with people in the church.

Scripture says, "If I give all I possess to the poor … but have not love, I gain nothing" (1

Corinthians 13:3). Love cannot be demonstrated *without relationships*. Merely *providing things* is not enough. The question then becomes for each church, "*How* do we base our outreach to the poor on relationships?"

It is easier to understand *why* many of our church-based outreach ministries among the poor have became rooted in providing things when we look at the growth of the welfare state in the last 60 years. It replaced caring parishioners with time-strapped social workers. In addition, the welfare state redirected churchgoers' tax dollars to support government programs rather than letting them support their own churches' outreach to the poor. The welfare state also gave away things to care for people's external needs and usurped the church's role of providing things as an opening to better care for people's internal needs.

The good news is our churches are at a crossroads in our outreach among the poor. Welfare as we knew it ended a few years ago. As noted in *The Welfare of My Neighbor: Living Out Christ's Love for the Poor*, our public policies have made necessary changes to make way for the good work of churches again. It is widely understood today that no other group can provide relationships and hope for the poor like our churches can. And most welfare families are looking for a new life that only churches can help them find.

We are also at the dawn of a new millennium, with all the hope, anticipation and excitement that brings. Many of our churches are examining the way we do things and especially whether we are reaching our neighbors with the good news of Jesus Christ. Many also are revising vision statements to include "reaching the world for Christ in the 21st century." This is a time for new ideas that are rooted in the principles of Scripture and the lessons learned from the 20th century. On the positive side, these lessons include recognizing the richness of relationships centered within churches. However, they also include the sobering realization of the distancing that has occurred between the very poor and suburban-based congregations and ministries.

This workbook will help you transition your church-based outreach ministries to reach the poor in America more effectively in the 21st century. Most of the contributors to this work are Christians on the front lines of ministry among the poor daily. They understand that the landscape for serving the poor has changed with the ending of "welfare as we knew it." They understand, also, the need to change "church-based outreach as we have known it" for the last 60 years. This is a change that is firmly grounded in the permanence of biblical truths presented in Scripture. This is also a change that depends on relationships centered on Jesus Christ.

In particular, this workbook will help your church establish a church-based mentoring ministry among welfare families. This type of ministry is much like my "core group," where a volunteer leader or leaders meets with a set group of people for a predetermined amount of time. This type of relational ministry is based on both the Word of God and on people, and it expects both the givers and the receivers to be transformed through their participation.

What makes this church-based mentoring model unique is that it is about building committed relationships with those *outside the church on government welfare*. There are over 3 million families on welfare today who are looking for this type of assistance from churches. Welfare moms and dads would be the first to admit that they need churches to give them a new life, not merely canned goods or motel vouchers. They desire committed relationships with those who value their very souls, not just the idea of changing their external circumstances.

This workbook is a supplement to the book *The Welfare of My Neighbor: Living Out Christ's Love for the Poor*. In the book, you are exposed to the idea of knowing and loving your neighbors who are currently on, or have recently escaped, government welfare. The state of welfare reform and that of church-based outreach are more fully explained in the book. Also, several ministries and resources are highlighted that can help your church expand its current outreach ministries in the context of welfare reform.

In this supplement, you will learn how to establish a church-based welfare-to-work mentoring ministry. This supplement is one of a kind, and I believe it contains the best wisdom and advice that currently exists from Christian practitioners for establishing relational ministry with welfare families outside the church. It shows us very practical steps to getting started today.

Thanks to this fine work by Amy Sherman (with others' shared expertise), there is a model for ministering to the needy outside the church that is rooted in our relationships both with each other and with Jesus Christ. I believe this model for ministry will make our churches more like Christ and that this is the future of church-based outreach ministry among the poor.

Deanna Lynn Carlson
Washington, D.C.
June 1999

Introduction

As explained in *The Welfare of My Neighbor: Living Out Christ's Love for the Poor*, ministry to the poor is not only a biblically mandated responsibility of the church but also a channel of blessing for the church. In other words, outreach to welfare recipients transforms both the welfare recipients and the church volunteers. For the church volunteer, this transformation is largely manifested through more meaningful worship of God. Our vision of God becomes enlarged as we share our lives with the lives of people in circumstances very foreign to our own. This happens when we witness God's acting in other people's lives in ways that may be unfamiliar to us. We see new facets of who God is and different kinds of deeds that He does that we may have otherwise missed. We can have a too-limited view of God's providence when our fellowship remains homogenous. For invigorated worship, we need to mingle with people whose prayer requests are very, very different from our own. When we are cut off from people with life situations unlike ours, we fail to learn how God gifts and graces those in circumstances unfamiliar to us — for example, being persecuted or discriminated against, being healed from crack addiction, or obtaining a job after 16 years on welfare. When we are in relationships with people who are praying for God's deliverance and provision in ways that we have never prayed before — and no one we've ever known has prayed before — and then we see God answer those prayers, we get a whole new glimpse of the wonderful deeds of the Lord. We see more clearly the *multifaceted* grace and provision of our heavenly Father, and our adoration of Him deepens.

Once your congregation is persuaded of the necessity — and the blessing — of embracing needy families affected by welfare reform, some reassessment of the church's previous mercy ministry efforts is required. If the congregation's involvement in mercy ministry has been limited to traditional, "commodity-based" benevolence (giving people who are poor food, clothing, and money), some changes are needed. While commodity-based benevolence is legitimate in certain cases, it can be misguided in others. Temporary relief assistance is valuable in situations where families have experienced an unexpected crisis, such as a house fire. However, when relief is merely a "Band-Aid" that alleviates the symptoms of poverty but fails to address the root causes, then it is illegitimate. Such assistance merely helps people to *manage* their poverty rather than to *escape* from it. When we are dealing with the able-bodied poor who experience chronic financial instability, then cash and commodities are inadequate.

What's needed is *church-based relational ministry* that provides a hand up to self-sufficiency. Of course, this type of ministry demands much more from us — not necessarily more of our money (though that may be true), but more of ourselves and our time. Commodity-based benevolence allows us to interact with poor people at arm's length. By contrast, church-based relational ministry is much less clinical and sterile. As the Church father Gregory of Nyssa said many centuries ago, "Mercy is a voluntary sorrow that joins itself to the suffering of another." Clearly this kind of mercy requires entangling our lives with the lives of the poor. It involves more than being willing to *help* the poor; it means being willing to *know* them.

Amy L. Sherman
Director of Urban Ministries, Trinity Presbyterian Church
Adjunct Fellow, The Manhattan Institute

Chapter One

ASSESSING YOUR CHURCH'S OUTREACH TO THE POOR

Effective church-based relational ministry among the poor begins with church leaders evaluating where they are currently in their outreach ministries. Most churches are doing good work, but they must determine if they are doing the best work they can. Below are critical areas of outreach that church leaders must address. Also, two assessment tools follow that have been used successfully by church leaders in their self-assessments of their churches and outreach ministries.

Church leaders must **study the Scriptures** to see what they say about helping the poor and needy. There are over 400 Bible verses about poverty; in fact, poverty is mentioned in the Bible more often than money. Yet many pastoral education programs do not include a course on God's heart for the poor. Thus, it is extremely vital that church leaders undergo some soul-searching or participate in a small-group study to understand God's perspective on the people they are or will be serving.

Church leaders must then *evaluate* their current outreach ministries to see whether these are truly helping needy people to transform their lives. Sometimes, as mentioned in the Introduction, we've been guilty of helping poor people to manage, rather than to escape, their poverty. Are our benevolence efforts engendering dependency or encouraging self-sufficiency? Are the same people coming back repeatedly for aid? What follow-up are we doing with recipients of aid? In what ways are we addressing the emotional and spiritual needs of those families?

Church leaders also need to *rethink* the scope of their efforts. Many congregations have fallen into the trap of "bigger is better." They offer multiple outreach programs that are a mile wide but only an inch deep. They're offering commodities to the poor, but not personal relationships with the poor. Churches that want to make a positive, sustainable difference in needy families' lives must begin to think "narrow and deep": that is, limiting the number of families served in order to more effectively and genuinely serve those that are helped.

The church must also ***define a philosophy*** for outreach ministry. This philosophy articulates the key principles or core values that will undergird the church's outreach work. The church will need to identify the different strategies that will be employed in its benevolence efforts, according to the nature of each needy family's particular situation (the disabled may need charity; families in temporary crisis, such as fire victims, might need groceries and shelter; the able-bodied poor may need job training or assistance with transportation or child care). The church should also articulate policies guiding the church's financial benevolence.

Church leaders should also ***assess what percentage*** of the congregation is involved in community outreach ministry. In order to mobilize a greater number of parishioners, church leaders must emphasize a vision of community ministry as "mutually transforming." We should expect that church volunteers who engage in ministry will be enriched and transformed through their service. We want, for example, to see church volunteers growing in their faith and their dependency on God; identifying and utilizing their spiritual gifts; confronting and overcoming their own prejudices; growing in gratitude; and deepening in their worship of Jesus, the suffering servant.

Tool One:
Your Church's Foundation
for Social Ministry

By Heidi Rolland Unruh

This exercise can help your church reflect on some of the factors that can affect the direction, effectiveness and sustainability of social ministry, and to discover areas needing to be strengthened, clarified, or changed as part of the process of developing outreach ministry. *Together with a group of people from your congregation, answer the following questions about your church. Then answer the reflection questions at the end.*

I. Vision for outreach ministry

1. Does your church have a mission statement? How is this mission communicated to the congregation? How is a vision for outreach expressed in church services, printed church brochures and handouts, etc.?

2. How does your church balance nurturing the congregation and reaching out to the community? Which is a higher priority, and why?

3. What goals or outcomes of social ministry would your church like to see: (a) For the individuals served? (b) For the community as a whole? (c) For your church itself? Which of these are the most important?

II. Theology for mission

4. What does your church believe are the main biblical or theological reasons for outreach?

5. Does the church believe that social ministries should share the Gospel? Offer prayer or spiritual counseling? Invite people to attend the church? Invite people to become a Christian? How do these happen in practice?

6. What do you think most helps needy people: Personal transformation? Supportive relationships? More opportunities for economic advancement? Better public policies? What is the church's role in these areas?

III. Leadership development

7. What are the most important qualities for leaders of social ministries? What kinds of support do program leaders need to be most effective?

8. What opportunities exist for the training of church leaders, ministry leaders and ministry volunteers? How are the pastor(s) involved in this process?

9. How do you tell if your training programs and processes of leadership development are effective?

IV. Organization for ministry

10. How has the church's organizational structure changed over the last ten years, and what were the reasons?

11. What responsibilities take up most of church leaders' time? What activities do leaders most want to be doing?

12. What processes for evaluation, accountability, and conflict management are in place?

V. Relationships between the congregation and community

13. What community events or programs has the church participated in? In what other ways does the church help people in the congregation get to know people outside the church?

14. How do you think someone in the neighborhood might describe your church?

15. What are the main changes taking place in the community? How has the church been affected by these changes, and how has it responded?

Reflection Questions:

For all of your answers above, discuss:

16. How might this information suggest a strength or a weakness of your church for social ministry?

17. How might this information relate to opportunities in the community for ministry?

18. How might your answers point to areas in the church that need to be more clearly or explicitly defined?

19. How can your church follow up on these reflections?

Heidi Rolland Unruh is associate director of the Congregations, Community, and Leadership Development Project of Evangelicals for Social Action in Philadelphia, Pa.

Tool Two:
How Is Your Church Doing in Making a Change in Your Neighbor's Welfare?

By Jenny Forner

Circle the number that best describes your church.

Guide: 10 – not at all; 20 – some; 30 – average; 40 – good; 50 – excellent

Our Church has ...

1. lots of small groups meeting at least twice a month	10	20	30	40	50
2. wonderful prayer support for each other	10	20	30	40	50
3. contact every week with its neighbors in some way	10	20	30	40	50
4. current leaders mentoring leaders who will succeed them	10	20	30	40	50
5. a reputation in the community as a caring place for hurting people	10	20	30	40	50
6. a system for members to learn how God wants us to spend money	10	20	30	40	50
7. a way to celebrate what God is doing through various members	10	20	30	40	50
8. each person writing how God has worked in his/her life (testimony)	10	20	30	40	50
9. a system to bring meals and care to members of our church	10	20	30	40	50
10. a prayer telephone line, listing prayer needs for the week	10	20	30	40	50
11. a place for people to come with physical needs (food, housing, $)	10	20	30	40	50
12. opportunities to develop leadership skills	10	20	30	40	50
13. groups of people who do projects in the community monthly	10	20	30	40	50

14. the resources we need to do the ministry God calls us to	10	20	30	40	50
15. a process through which all members discover their gifts and are interviewed about where to serve	10	20	30	40	50
16. a way for people to build relationships with the poor	10	20	30	40	50
17. the reputation of being a place where you are loved	10	20	30	40	50
18. been growing in its prayer life, corporately and individually	10	20	30	40	50
19. included people who receive food, etc., in work projects	10	20	30	40	50
20. church leaders' quarterly ongoing education and support meetings	10	20	30	40	50
21. many of its families involved weekly with one person who has needs	10	20	30	40	50
22. over 50% of our families giving God 10% of what He has given them	10	20	30	40	50
23. over 50% of our families serving regularly in some ministry capacity	10	20	30	40	50
24. the joy of hearing what God is doing in our lives regularly	10	20	30	40	50

Place the answer for each question on the appropriate line.

Church Family	Prayer	Being Open	Leadership Development
1. _____	2. _____	3. _____	4. _____
9. _____	10. _____	11. _____	12. _____
17. _____	18. _____	19. _____	20. _____
_____	_____	_____	_____
Total	Total	Total	Total

Outreach	Finances	Volunteer Management	Sharing Our Testimony
5. _____	6. _____	7. _____	8. _____
13. _____	14. _____	15. _____	16. _____
21. _____	22. _____	23. _____	24. _____
_____	_____	_____	_____
Total	Total	Total	Total

The highest scoring items reflect the strengths of your church.

What are your church's greatest strengths?

1.

2.

What are the weak areas?

Jesus' two greatest commandments are:

"Love the Lord your God, with all your heart and mind, and your neighbor as yourself."

1.

2.

What three steps do you need to begin the process?

1.

2.

3.

Jenny Forner is the founder and executive director of New Focus, a Christ-centered, church-based mentoring ministry for the poor in Allendale, Mich. Established in 1994, New Focus helps churches to utilize "knock on the door" requests to move the poor to financial independence and spiritual growth through long-term relationships with church members.

Chapter Two

ADVANCING YOUR CHURCH'S OUTREACH TO THE POOR

Once the congregation has studied God's heart for the poor, articulated its own vision and philosophy of outreach, and assessed its current efforts, several practical steps to "get going" can be taken. The sequence of these steps will vary, depending on the unique characteristics of the congregation and its articulated vision for ministry. Here are some typical steps churches take:

1. *Assessing the church's strengths and weaknesses.* Identify the church's assets and resources it can share with the needy. Take inventory of the congregation's talents.

2. *Learning about the local community and its socio-economic needs*.

3. *Assessing what services are already being provided.* Who is providing them? Where are there gaps? Are there existing Christian ministries with which the church can partner?

4. *Building relationships in neighborhoods of need.* Identify Christian brothers and sisters in economically distressed communities. Meet and pray with them, and learn their own assessment of their community and its assets and needs. Find out what vision they may have for serving their community and how your church can work with them to help.

5. *Gathering a core working team composed of church leaders, laity, and members of the community.* The working team can assess the community's needs

and identify what unique niche the church may be able to fill. The team can also study models of other church-based community ministries, learn from these, and adapt the "best practices" to their own particular situation.

6. ***Establishing a system for recruiting, screening, training, placing, and shepherding volunteers.*** (See Appendix A.) Write up "job descriptions" of volunteer positions. Run a class on "identifying your spiritual gifts" and, at its conclusion, have representatives of the church's outreach ministries make presentations about service opportunities they can offer. Find a church member who can serve as the ministry's "Volunteer Coordinator." Write up "volunteer applications" that can serve as screening mechanisms (Note: For outreach to youth, it's very important to have volunteers provide personal references). Hold "ministry fairs" that showcase the church's different service ministries. Think creatively about how existing fellowship groups within the congregation (e.g., the Ladies Prayer Circle, a Sunday School class, the youth group, or the Men's Bible Study) can serve *as groups* in the outreach ministry.

Overcoming the Barriers to Reaching Out

Church leaders must be prepared to help church members overcome various external and internal barriers to reaching out. Some common barriers include the following:

- Our reluctance to go where needy people are
- Cultural, racial, and class divides that we need to cross
- Our tendency not to want to help those whose sin has contributed to their present dilemma
- Our reluctance to be personally inconvenienced
- Our busyness

Some effective ways of overcoming these barriers include activities that expose church members to needy neighborhoods (see Chapter 9: "Service Trips in the United States," in *The Welfare of My Neighbor*); teaching principles of racial reconciliation; teaching congregants to meditate on the truth that each member of the Body "belongs" to all the others (Romans 12:5); embracing God's promise that if we spend ourselves on behalf of the poor and needy, He will make us "well-watered gardens" (Isaiah 58:10-11); and encouraging congregants to assess their "time-styles," reevaluate their priorities, and create room in their schedules for service.

Chapter Three

UNLEASHING RELATIONAL MINISTRIES AMONG WELFARE FAMILIES

Although numerous models of relational ministries exist, welfare-to-work mentoring ministries are perhaps the type most needed in this era of welfare reform. This is a type of ministry that capitalizes on one of the Church's greatest strengths: its people, with their love, faith, talents, social networks, and life experiences. Churches interested in establishing this type of relational ministry should mobilize a "start-up committee" to lead the mentoring initiative. The committee's first job is to wrestle with four key questions about the nature of the proposed mentoring program.

1. What kinds of mentoring will our church focus on?

The first key question the start-up committee must think through involves the two different kinds of mentoring situations: *Will the mentoring effort focus primarily on individuals who do not yet have jobs or on individuals who have obtained employment but need help in retaining their jobs and planning for their future?* A church can decide to embrace one or the other, or both kinds of program participants, but the objectives of the mentoring teams are distinct in each case.

The team working with an individual with no job will focus on such issues as the development of job readiness skills, writing a résumé, practicing job interviews, identifying potential job opportunities, and making child-care and transportation arrangements. However, most organizations involved in job training report that finding an individual a new job is not as difficult as helping to ensure that the individual retains the job. The team working with an individual who has already secured a job will want to focus on two main areas: job retention and "personal strategic planning."

Regarding job retention, the team and the participant should identify potential problems that could jeopardize the participant's ability to retain his or her current position. Mentoring teams can help prepare the participant to cope appropriately with potential on-the-job problems, such as how to relate to a difficult boss or co-workers or irate customers. The team should also help the participant strategize about balancing family and work effectively. Most employees struggle with this question, particularly single mothers with children too young to look after themselves. Mentoring teams can discuss with their participants at least three relevant issues in this regard: (1) strategies for discussing with the supervisor arrangements for dealing with pressing family/child matters that require time away from the job; (2) assessing when something is really a "family crisis" that requires leaving work and when the situation must wait for the parent's attention until after work hours; and (3) planning ahead for child-care contingencies (What will the parent do, for instance, if the regular babysitter can't watch the kids? What are his or her plan A and plan B for when a child is sick on a workday?).

Regarding "personal strategic planning," the team and the participant should develop a plan that will place the participant in a position of greater job and financial stability within the next two years. The time limits set on welfare benefits (in most states, two years of continuous assistance and a lifetime cap of five years' assistance) mean that individuals in financially precarious situations must carefully and deliberately decide when to "lean on" such aid and when to struggle along without it, reserving the possibility of getting aid at a future time when it may be more needed. Welfare reform was aimed in part at encouraging recipients' greater economic self-sufficiency through work. The first job a recipient is able to secure, however, may not provide an income adequate to meet the family's legitimate expenses. Consequently, the participant must think beyond the first job. The participant and the team can discuss such important questions as: How much income do I need to provide for myself and my family? Is there room for advancement in the job I have just secured? How can I be training myself and enhancing my job skills now so that in another year I will be in a position to obtain a higher-paying job? Should I continue to receive welfare benefits now that I have obtained employment, or should I try to make it without public assistance now so that I may rely on it in the future if needed? Helping the participant to develop a workable monthly budget — and stick to it — can also be a critical objective of the mentoring relationship.

2. Will we pursue team mentoring or a one-on-one model?

While a few churches have run effective mentoring programs that utilize a one-on-one approach, most employ a team approach. It can be easier to mobilize volunteers when they realize that they will not be alone in the ministry to the participant. Team ministry helps protect volunteers from "burnout." It also increases the number of contacts the participant can lean upon in his or her job search. A team will also have a broader diversity of gifts and life experiences to share with the participant. On the other hand, the one-on-one approach may be less overwhelming to the participant, since it requires him or her to build a relationship with just one person. Some churches have utilized a hybrid approach: putting one individual in the "front-line" relationship with the participant, but mobilizing a small support team around that front-line mentor. This team stays in the background, but is available to help the front-line mentor with tasks he or she cannot do. For example, the front-line mentor may learn that the participant's child needs a tutor and that the participant's car needs repairing. Rather than trying to provide help alone, the front-line mentor asks the support team to step in to meet those specific needs or to identify other people in the church who could help.

3. Will the mentoring relationship involve any financial assistance from the church to the participant?

Study of church-based mentoring models around the country indicates that churches have widely differing experiences in this area. Some provide no financial assistance to the participant whatsoever and believe that the introduction of money can negatively influence the mentoring relationship. Other churches provide outright grants to the participant, sometimes in amounts greater than $1000. Still others have integrated no-interest loans into the participant's overall strategy for greater economic self-reliance. Others have provided non-monetary aid to program participants (for example, used household goods, furniture, or clothing) or have subsidized participants' rent or child-care expenses through direct payments to the providers.

Should the church decide that it is willing to include financial assistance as part of the "package" of support for the participant, some important guidelines should be kept in mind (see side text).

Be *creative* in your use of the church's financial assistance and think through ways that the money can be used strategically as an *investment* in the participant's future, rather than as a stopgap to deal with a current crisis. Money given to repair the person's car or to pay for a training course is typically better than money given to pay the person's furniture rental bill.

Or, suppose a participant has a long record of public assistance and little or no solid work history. Consider using church funds to underwrite a paid internship. Contact local nonprofit organizations to see if they would be willing

> ## Suggested Guidelines for Financial Assistance
>
> 1. Decide on a ceiling amount of assistance.
> 2. Communicate clearly to the participant what your financial aid policies are.
> 3. Never give money directly to the participant; rather, pay service providers (e.g., landlord, utility company, creditors) directly.
> 4. Decide in advance what constitutes a legitimate expenditure and under what conditions the church will provide financial aid.
> 5. Be able to answer the question: How will this financial aid contribute to the achievement of the participant's overall plan for greater economic self-reliance? (How is this gift or loan part of a larger, clearly defined strategy for help?)
> 6. Financial assistance should usually be given in conjunction with budget counseling.

to be a placement site for such "work experience internships." These internships cost them nothing financially, since the church is providing the funds for the participant's stipend. The participant earns the stipend by his or her work at the internship site; thus it is not a handout. Potential internship placements should be selected on the basis of what new skills training they would offer to the participant (e.g., will there be an opportunity to learn how to manage a multi-line phone, learn new computer applications or practice typing skills?) The nonprofit should also agree to supervise the intern and provide a formal, written evaluation of his or her performance at the conclusion of the internship. If the participant's performance is good, he or she will be in a better position to enter the labor market, having in hand a positive recommendation and a steady period of employment. (It is best to set the internship up on a less than 40 hours/week basis — say 30 hours — to allow the participant some weekday time to engage in job search activities and interviews.)

Churches can also design ways of using financial aid as an incentive for positive change. For example, suppose a program participant has come to see the value of getting out of debt. The church might encourage the participant to use disposable income to start paying debts (as opposed to increasing current expenditures) by agreeing to match each dollar he or she puts toward repayment. Or, if the individual has developed a budget that calls for saving $10 per week in a "rainy day fund," the church can offer to match his or her savings efforts for the first few months.

4. What will be the basic structure of the mentoring relationship?

To be effective, the mentoring program must be built on a more specific and concrete strategy than merely "being the participant's friend." Obviously, the mentors should befriend the participant and work diligently at developing an open, honest, caring, and supportive relationship marked by winsomeness and humility. But mentoring should aim at achieving various well-defined objectives. These could include developing a monthly budget, writing a résumé, completing a certain number of job interviews, taking the GED test, enrolling in a computer training class, identifying affordable day care, developing a plan to get out of debt, going to informational interviews, moving into more affordable housing, and purchasing a reliable used car.

The church should decide the *length of the commitment* required of the mentors. Most programs I have studied involve at least a six months' commitment; others require a one-year commitment. Also, the leaders of the mentoring program should *develop a basic "covenant"* to be used with each team and participant. This covenant outlines the responsibilities and expectations of both parties. The specific details of the covenant will be unique to each participant and team, but all covenants should include the minimum expectation of the participant's agreement to meet face-to-face on a regular basis with the team (I recommend at least once every two weeks) and to be honest with them. The team members and the participant should jointly *formulate an "action plan"* that will guide their work together. The action plan should be based on a careful assessment of the participant's needs, assets, and goals. The plan should state the specific objectives sought (e.g., completing a résumé) and the timeline for achieving them. The plan will then serve as an overall road map to guide the team in its relationship with the participant. A good covenant is one that communicates clearly the role of the mentoring team (what they will and will not do) and the responsibilities of the participant. In this way, the expectations are clearly communicated from the beginning. The covenant and action plan then also serve as a basis of accountability and of demarcating the participant's overall progress.

Chapter Four[1]

TEN STEPS TO ESTABLISHING A MENTORING MINISTRY

STEP 1: CONNECTING WITH A WELFARE FAMILY

Partnering with a parachurch ministry.

Many congregations desire to serve needy families, but don't know where they live or how to establish a relationship with them. One of the functions of the start-up committee is to investigate potential partnerships that can link church members with families making the transition from welfare to work. Local Christian parachurch ministries serving the poor are a great place to start. The committee should identify any local Christian ministries with whom the church can partner that are engaged with specific families needing assistance. The Salvation Army and Love INC are two examples of such potential partners. See Chapters 8 and 10 in *The Welfare of My Neighbor* for a listing of such ministries.

Partnering with the department of social services.

In the absence of these kinds of organizations, the start-up committee could approach the local department of social services (DSS) to inquire whether it would be interested in establishing a welfare-to-work mentoring program. Such church-state partnerships are already underway in Mississippi (the Faith and Families Program), Michigan (Project Zero), South Carolina (Putting Families First), and many other states (see Chapter 8 in *The Welfare of My Neighbor*). Welfare reform has created new incentives for local governments to turn to the faith community for help in transitioning families from welfare to work. Many caseworkers know that they cannot provide individualized, time-intensive assistance to each of their clients when they are carrying a caseload of 40 or 50 individuals. Thus, many welcome the support of mentors from the churches who can invest significant time and care in the lives of their clients. An effective partnership with the local DSS can be pursued if several conditions are met (see Appendix B for discussion of this topic).

[1] Much information in this chapter is drawn from Good Samaritan Ministries' manual, *Building Transformational Relationships with Low-Income Families.* See Chapter 8 in *The Welfare of My Neighbor* for more information.

Transcending Racial Divides

Faye Lucius from Mississippi was part of a small team that worked for a year with "Mary," a highly motivated welfare recipient. She reports that she has learned much from Mary about contentment and gratitude to God. Also, Faye says she grew up in a family that was prejudiced toward African-Americans. She appreciated the opportunity to build a close friendship with an African-American woman, and the chance her children have had to develop friendships with Mary's children. "I've never wanted my children to be uncomfortable around black kids. I've taught them that God loves everybody, that we're all the same in God's eyes. My kids enjoy our visits with [Mary] and her kids, and they are seeing that blacks and whites can get along.

"I recognize that, but for the grace of God, I could easily be in [Mary's] situation," Faye says. "[The friendship with Mary] got me out of my comfort zone. I'd helped with other benevolence type projects, but this involved more personal interaction. And getting involved personally makes you think of all that God has done for you. Churches need to be involved in this kind of face-to-face [ministry]."

Partnering with an urban or rural church.

Most churches located in rural and urban neighborhoods have welfare families either in their congregations or at their doorsteps. Suburban churches can minister to welfare families by establishing a partnership with an urban or rural church. This type of church-church partnership brings Christians, often of different races, together for greater impact. When churches of different races come together for the benefit of the poor, they not only minister to the people served, but they also communicate to the wider community a powerful love, rooted in Christ, that transcends racial divides. This is also a tremendous opportunity for a suburban church to practice the humility required for this type of partnership and for an urban or rural church to renew its trust in suburban churches. For more information on this type of partnership, see Chapters 6 and 8 (see "National Jobs Partnership" and "STEP") in *The Welfare of My Neighbor* and Appendix D in this supplement.

Adopting a family the church has assisted in the past.

A fourth way of linking church-based mentoring teams with families on welfare is to pursue relationships with specific families the church has assisted in the past. For example, the church may have records of families that have recently received financial assistance or groceries. These families can be contacted to see whether the head of the household is affected by welfare reform and if he or she would like to discuss the possibility of receiving help from the church while making the transition off public assistance.

Adopting a family that requests assistance from the church.

The church can adopt a new benevolence policy under which families that request financial assistance are screened for potential involvement in a mentoring program. Several churches, with the help of a Christian organization called New Focus, have successfully "remodeled" their traditional financial benevolence programs into systems for conducting relational, holistic ministry. Under the New Focus system, families requesting aid from the church are invited to a short meeting in which they can learn about the New Focus program and decide whether they want to work with church members to design a personalized strategy for achieving greater financial stability through employment and wise family budgeting. (See Chapter 8 in *The Welfare of My Neighbor* and Appendix C in this supplement for descriptions of New Focus.)

STEP 2: RECRUITING MENTORS

Promotion in the church.

The start-up committee is also responsible for designing a system to promote the mentoring program and recruit mentors. In most instances, lay mobilization will be easier if the church's senior pastor is a vocal supporter of the mentoring initiative. The pastor need not be involved personally in the day-to-day activities of the mentoring program, but his public support of the initiative will usually help recruiting efforts. The pastor can legitimize the outreach in the eyes of the average pew-sitter, and can exhort the laity to service. The start-up committee should utilize whatever communication vehicles are available to promote the new mentoring initiative: the church newsletter, the Sunday bulletin, a bulletin board, display booths, and so on.

Engaging small groups.

One helpful principle of volunteer recruitment is to design ways for existing groups within the congregation to serve *as groups*. Our church, for example, has a large number of "home fellowship groups," small groups of 5-10 people who meet regularly for prayer, Bible study, and fellowship. The individuals involved already know and enjoy one another, and they may be more willing to serve as a mentoring team because they see such service as an opportunity to deepen their relationships and to stretch and grow as a group. An adult Sunday school class that breaks into small prayer or discussion groups or a women's weekly prayer circle are other potential pools of mentoring teams. (For further tips on volunteer recruitment, see Appendix A.)

A Better Return on the Church's Investment

Tom, the business manager at a "mega-church" in Michigan, reports that prior to adopting a mentoring approach to working with low-income families, "we knew we weren't doing a good job of really addressing people's problems. We were just helping to take care of the symptoms. We didn't have a formal structure in place to walk families through whatever particular crisis they were in — there wasn't a lot of ongoing contact with the people, there wasn't much accountability. Now we are able to really get alongside people and encourage and counsel them, give them direction and advice, and sometimes correct them if necessary. Now we're seeing visible changes in families' lives. They're making good progress getting out of debt, we're seeing them feel better about themselves, we're seeing positive results. We're seeing a better return on our investment [of benevolence money]. The families have never had any one care about them or be concerned about them, and now someone is. That has made them want to become a part of what's going on here at Calvary [the church]. So we're seeing them become part of our different programs, coming under some teaching so they can grow in their spiritual journey."

STEP 3: TRAINING MENTORS

Gathering appropriate training materials and trainers.

One individual on the start-up committee should lay the groundwork for the training program that will be necessary once several congregants have volunteered to serve as mentors. This will involve (a) identifying good trainers, either inside or outside the church, and (b) gathering appropriate training materials (including information on cross-cultural ministry, active listening skills, problem-solving skills, and how to avoid volunteer burnout). See Chapters 8 and 10 in *The Welfare of My Neighbor* for lists of ministries and additional resources.

Reviewing administrative details.

There are several mundane but nonetheless important details that every mentor needs to know, such as time commitment expected from mentors; key dates for meetings; where meetings will be held (include directions to the meeting site); and where to park.

Mentors may also have questions about liability. For example, what happens if the mentor is driving the participant to a job interview and they get involved in a car accident in which the participant is injured? The start-up committee should already have discussed such liability issues and checked with the church administrator to get an overview of the church's liability insurance policy. The church may need to add a rider to its general insurance policy that covers accidents in vehicles utilized by church members who are conducting a service (e.g., giving the participant a ride to a job interview) under the auspices of the church.

It is best to distribute written handouts with the basic information a mentor will need (telephone numbers for contacting the program director and start-up committee members, a list of key dates, and so on). That way, the mentors carry home from the training an informational reference guide that they can consult as needed.

STEP 4: PROVIDING STRUCTURE TO THE MENTORING RELATIONSHIP

While just "being a friend" is critical to the effectiveness of any mentoring program, it is usually inadequate by itself. The mentoring relationship typically feels awkward at first, because it begins between strangers who, at least initially, may be more focused on their dissimilarities than on their similarities. Even as the relationship grows, the mentor may feel uncertain about his or her role if certain minimum expectations are not specified. The mentoring relationship should be a *directed friendship,* and it needs a certain amount of structure in order to flourish. Specifically, there should be in place a means of spiritual discipleship and of socio-economic improvement. The program participant should be on a journey towards "true sufficiency"; in other words, he or she should be engaged in taking steps to increase his or her economic self-reliance and understanding of God's providence and care.

If the mentoring component is part of a larger training program operated by the church's partner agency, then the church itself need not create a lot of structure.

For example, in our city, the Salvation Army operates a program called "Project Breakthrough." Low-income residents enroll in Project Breakthrough and attend weekly classes at the Salvation Army facility covering such topics as job readiness and family budgeting. The Project Breakthrough staff person enjoys regular contact with the program participants and is available for informal counseling and advice. Churches participate in Project Breakthrough by providing mentor teams. Each team is matched with a program participant and cheers the participant through the program. After the participant graduates from Project

Breakthrough's classes, the mentor team continues to meet regularly with him or her to provide tailored assistance according to the action plan the participant, the mentor team, and the Project Breakthrough staff person have designed.

If the mentoring component is not a part of a larger training program, the church itself may need to create the structure for training and support.

In our church's ministry, called JobKEYS, Friendship Circles play a similar role to that played by church mentor teams involved with Project Breakthrough. Church staff members operate the "structured" part of the JobKEYS program. This involves a six-week, biblically based life skills class (which includes lessons on personal budgeting), an 18-week course in basic word processing, and several job readiness seminars (on such topics as "Balancing Family and Work" and "Effective Interviewing").

Participants in the JobKEYS program are introduced to their Friendship Circle mentors about four weeks into the program. The first meeting is held at the facility where the computer classes are taught. Circles and their assigned participants get acquainted for thirty minutes over coffee and doughnuts. Then, on the final day of the life skills course, the Circles and the JobKEYS participants all go out for lunch.

The next week, the JobKEYS participants attend a workshop on "personal strategic planning," where they are encouraged to write down their personal assets and liabilities, as well as brainstorm about their goals and their needs. They also complete a "job needs and preferences" questionnaire that summarizes their career interests, work background, type of job environment they think they would do well in, and desired salary and work schedule. These activities help prepare them for their first "working session" with the Friendship

The start-up phase of the welfare-to-work mentoring program is complete when ...

- The whole initiative is undergirded in prayer.
- The church has partnered with an organization that can screen potential participant families and refer them to the church, or has developed its own participant recruitment and screening procedure.
- The pastor has encouraged congregants to support the new initiative in whatever ways they can — by being mentors or prayer warriors or joining in the large "support services" network standing behind the "front-line" mentors.
- The start-up committee has a clear idea of the nature and goals of the mentoring program and is prepared to oversee the initiative (i.e., be the liaison with the partnering agency; shepherd, advise, encourage, and evaluate the mentor teams; and report on the initiative to church leaders).
- The congregation is truly mobilized for action. Church members are aware of the new initiative. Mentors have stepped forward and are beginning their training.
- The church has thought through its financial assistance guidelines and has determined the length and nature of the mentoring relationship.
- The start-up committee has renewed the church's liability insurance and made any necessary additions to cover volunteer mentors working under the church's auspices. (For example, the church may wish to purchase additional insurance covering volunteers who use their own vehicles to transport program participants.)

Circle. At that meeting, the participants and Circles flesh out an action plan to guide their work together over the next months.

In this model, the church is providing both the *training* component and the *support* component. Through the JobKEYS course, participants are introduced to biblical principles concerning work, time and money management, and family, and they learn marketable computer skills that enhance their prospects for obtaining jobs paying more than the minimum wage. Through the Friendship Circles, they enjoy the emotional and practical support of new friends who care about and respect them.

Not all churches have the financial and volunteer resources to provide both the training and the support components.

These churches do best to partner with some agency (preferably a Christian nonprofit) that offers a training program (like Project Breakthrough). Where no viable options for partnerships exist, the church should creatively consider how to incorporate some sort of "formal" instruction into the mentoring program.

STEP 5: BUILDING A MENTORING TEAM

Preparing for a multifaceted role.

The mentoring team should include a mix of "relationally oriented" people and "task-oriented" people. Part of the work of the team is to be good listeners, encouragers, and cheerleaders. Often, the participant will want to talk about issues that seem only indirectly related to the questions of finding and retaining a good job. It is important to keep in mind that these indirect issues (for example, difficulty collecting child support, a stressful relationship with a boyfriend, or a teenage child failing in school) consume enormous amounts of the participant's emotional energy, energy that is then not available for channeling into the job pursuit.

During the first year of our church's mentoring program, one mentor team found itself spending much time counseling its participant to break up with her abusive boyfriend. Another team spent many hours helping its participant work through the guilt she felt concerning an abortion she had had some years before. In both instances, members of the mentoring team wondered whether they were talking about the "right" issues with their participant, since these issues were not directly related to job goals. I encouraged them to remember that these issues were the ones on the participants' "front burners," and until they could be dealt with to some extent, the participants' ability to focus on "job-related pursuits" would be hindered. Team members who are more relationally oriented can help the participant work through whatever her "front burner" issues happen to be. As the participant feels secure and supported by those individuals, feeling that he or she does have someone to talk to, he or she will be better empowered to work constructively with the more task-oriented team members on concrete projects, such as résumés or job applications.

Building the mentor team.

The mentor team will minister more effectively if the team members have the opportunity to get acquainted before they meet the program participant with whom they will be matched. The team members should conduct an "inventory" to identify the special talents of each person and the role with which each would feel most comfortable, given his or her personality type. Some people are more relational and will be best used as encouragers and infor-

> The mentor team cannot "solve" all the participant's problems, nor should it even attempt to do so. The participant's ability to make progress in terms of greater economic self-reliance will be affected to some degree by his or her relationships with friends and neighbors, family life, health, and so forth. The mentor team must not be blind to the ways in which these facets of the participant's life help or hinder her progress in achieving the specific goals she and the team have formulated.

mal counselors. Other people are more task-oriented and will be most effective in assisting the participant to attain specific objectives, such as writing a résumé, developing a monthly budget or learning to drive. One person should serve as team secretary, taking notes at each meeting with the participant so that the mentors and participant clearly recall what plans they have set, what action steps the participants and the mentors will be taking the next week or two, and when the group will meet. Another individual can serve as the team's link to the broader congregation, and specifically to the "supportive services" organized by the start-up committee.

Good Samaritan Ministries in Holland, Mich., has been training churches in relational ministries for several years and is actively involved in assisting churches to establish welfare-to-work mentoring programs (see Chapter 8 in *The Welfare of My Neighbor* for more information on Good Samaritan Ministries). They have identified the main "functions" of the mentoring team as follows (not all mentoring teams need to be this large; this list is given as a guide to the typical roles different people on the mentoring teams play):

1. Team Leader(s):
   - Establishes primary relationship with the family
   - Communicates the needs of the family to the appropriate team members
   - Maintains regular contact with the family being mentored and with team members
   - Calls team meetings
   - Monitors overall morale of team members
   - Completes monthly planning agreements and progress reports and submits to the program director or start-up committee

2. Prayer Coordinator:
   - Organizes ongoing prayer for the team and the family being mentored
   - Leads devotional or prayer time prior to team meetings

3. Friend/Encourager:
   - A non-judgmental friend for the family to lean upon in time of need; someone who is

willing to exchange phone numbers so the family has someone to call and confide in. This person should be an encourager and able to motivate the family.

4. Volunteer/Support Services Coordinator:
- Helps find church resources to fill immediate needs (clothing, supplies)
- Acts as secretary during team meetings

5. Budget Counselor:
- Works with the participant in developing a workable monthly budget
- Reviews options for increasing income and decreasing expenses with participant

6. Employment Coordinator:
- Addresses obstacles to adequate employment (i.e., job training or résumé help needed)
- Assists parent(s) in arranging child care (daily care and "back up" care)
- Assists parent(s) with making long-term transportation arrangements

7. Education Coordinator:
- Assists parent(s) with enrolling in necessary educational or job skills training programs

8. Living Skills/Needs Coordinator:
- Assists family in finding long-term solutions for transportation, clothing, food, furniture
- Addresses legal and/or medical needs as they arise

Establishing Effective Teamwork

Good Samaritan Ministries also emphasizes the following important guidelines for effective teamwork:

1. "To speak the truth in love" is an expectation for all team members.
2. Team members should always communicate regularly with each other in order to promote consistency.
3. Team members should never do for the family what they can and want to do for themselves.
4. Team members must not be pitted against one another.
5. Team members should regularly re-evaluate their involvement in the ministry.
6. Team members should respect the family's privacy and not discuss their situation with other church members, family members, or friends without written permission from the family.
7. Team members should divide work responsibilities as evenly as possible.

Learning to relate across racial and class differences.

One of the first concerns some mentors have is that they have not built friendships before with someone from a different racial or ethnic background. Other mentors have had cross-cultural relationships, but not with individuals from a lower socio-economic status. Awareness of differences makes some mentors nervous about their relationship with the program participant. What follows are some suggestions from existing mentoring programs that may be helpful in alleviating that nervousness and equipping people for cross-cultural relationships.

1. Build on common elements. Perhaps the participant is a Christian; thus there is already a spiritual bond between the participant and the mentors. Find out the participant's hobbies or favorite sports teams or previous places of residence — these might also be possible points of connection. Or perhaps the participant has children who are similar in age to a mentor's children, or children who are engaged in the same kinds of activities. Remember that we have far more in common with others that we may initially recognize.

2. Keep the first two meetings between the participant and the mentoring team short. A half-hour "get-acquainted time" over coffee and doughnuts might be appropriate. The next meeting might then be a special lunch out or some other social activity, such as a picnic or a sports game. The third meeting between the participant and the mentoring team can be the first true "working session"; it will go more smoothly because a basic comfort level will already have been achieved.

The mentoring team should, prior to meeting the participant, examine themselves and ask God to cleanse them of any prejudices. The team will benefit greatly from reading a book on racial reconciliation from a Christian perspective.

STEP 6: ENGAGING THE ENTIRE CHURCH

Learning about available resources.

Once mentor teams are actively engaged in relationships with individuals making the transition from welfare to work, they will typically discover various needs that the larger church body could help meet. For example, the participant might need his or her car repaired, or a tutor to help him or her study for the GED, or training in computer skills, or some clothes appropriate for job interviewing. A member of the start-up committee should begin to "catalogue" the various support services church members could provide. This could be done in the form of a "Talents and Resources Survey" given to church members to complete. The survey would list various *talents* people have that they would be willing to share with the families being mentored (for example, ability to teach computer skills, ability to help someone prepare a résumé, mechanical ability) and various *resources* they could contribute to the families (business clothing, children's clothing, a car, a computer, or other items.)

Mobilizing a prayer support team for the ministry.

Design a "mentor support" system. Mobilize a prayer team to undergird the mentors in prayer and to organize regular — e.g., monthly or quarterly — mentor gatherings where mentors can swap information and experiences and can encourage and refresh one another. (If the church already has a Mothers of Preschoolers (MOPS) program in place, a leader from that ministry would make an excellent trainer.)

Maintaining the vision throughout the congregation.

To keep the church committed to and enthusiastic about the mentoring program, success stories should be shared regularly (through the church newsletter or a testimony in church by a mentor or participant). As the congregation hears these stories, more members may decide to sign up as mentors. Most importantly, the congregation is edified by hearing how God has been at work in the lives of the mentors and the program participants.

STEP 7: MONITORING THE MENTORING RELATIONSHIPS

The start-up committee is responsible for monitoring how the relationships between mentor teams and participants are going. If the church mentors several families, the committee may want to assign one of its members the role of "program director," or even hire an individual part-time to fulfill this job. Also, as mentioned earlier, mentor teams should assign a secretary for the group, taking notes at each meeting and keeping track of the participant's progress in reaching the goals outlined in his or her personal action plan. These notes should be shared with the start-up committee or program director. Depending on the closeness of the church's partnership with whatever agency referred the participant to the church's mentoring program (e.g., the department of social services), the mentoring team may also want to keep the participant's caseworker informed about the team's work with the participant.

STEP 8: RESOLVING CONFLICTS

Developing effective problem-solving skills.

One of the most important jobs of the mentoring team is to assist the participants in becoming effective problem solvers. This is a learned skill, not one that necessarily comes naturally. A person's ability to solve problems may depend in part on what sort of behavior was modeled before him or her. Some people were raised in homes where problems were simply ignored. Others grew up in homes where a "wait and see" attitude was always present in regard to problems — the hope that if they waited, time would eliminate the need for action. Still others find themselves so overwhelmed by the problem that even considering possible responses causes them to become almost paralyzed. Other people respond to problems by lashing out and blaming others. And still others turn to those around them for help and advice.

Being prepared to manage problems.

It is pleasant for me to be able to report that I have witnessed few problems in the mentoring efforts I have studied in several states. Nonetheless, conflicts sometimes do arise, and every mentor team must be prepared for the possibility of some tough times. The most common problem is that the participant loses motivation and begins missing meetings or failing to do the tasks he or she had agreed to do under the action plan. The first step in handling this sort of problem is for one or two people on the team to gently confront the participant and ask why he or she has missed meetings. The issue may be simply that the participant had legitimate reasons for missing (a child was sick, a ride fell through, and so on) and that he or she dropped the ball in calling the team members to inform them of what was going on. In this case, the participant should simply be encouraged to remember to call if he or she encounters a problem.

In other cases, it may be that the participant is going through something stressful that has sapped her motivation to work with the team. She may want to work with the team but

Good Samaritan Ministries suggests that mentor teams utilize the following five-point process for problem solving with their participants:

1. ***Listen to the stated problem.*** Team members should practice "active listening," that is, reflecting back to others what you understand them to be saying. It means communicating to the speaker that you are "tracking" with him or her.

2. ***Define the problem and identify possible causes.*** Having a clear, well-defined understanding of the problem aids in finding solutions. Problems can relate to lack of resources (money, job); lack of skills (in using a computer or managing money); lack of information (about where to shop or how to apply or interview effectively for a job); lack of support (from friends who can encourage or provide practical help, such as a ride to an interview); or lack of motivation (the failure to carry through decisions). Mentors should help the participant write short, clear, specific, objective problem statements: For example, rather than defining the problem as "financial difficulties," define it as "a $50-per-month shortfall between my income and my expenses."

3. ***Establish goals.*** Goal statements, like problem statements, should be clear, specific, and objective. Mentors should help participants identify "SMART" goals, that is, goals that are:
   *S*pecifically related to the problem;
   *M*easurable, not vague;
   *A*ttainable rather than unrealistic;
   *R*esults-oriented, rather than process-oriented;
   *T*ime-limited, rather than indefinite.

4. ***Plan a solution.***
   a) Generate alternatives — ask the participant how she thinks the goal can be reached. Ask what the participant has already tried, what his or her friends have suggested, and what he or she thinks would be helpful for achieving the goal.
   b) Evaluate the alternatives — Think aloud with the participant about the pros and cons of each suggestion. Ask whether a particular suggestion is possible, likely to be effective, and acceptable to the participant and his or her family.
   c) Develop a plan — A good plan is crafted with much input from the participant; it should not be imposed on the participant by the mentor team. It should be a detailed, step-by-step plan for tackling the problems the participant has defined and moving toward his or her goals. The complete plan will identify, for each action item, who is doing what by when.

5. ***Implement and evaluate.*** The mentor team should ask the participant for progress updates and hold the participant accountable for implementing different action items according to the time frame defined in the plan. The team should be a sounding board for the participant, as he or she confronts various obstacles to implementation or has to reconsider earlier decisions and/or change course. Remember that transformation usually comes in a long series of small steps. Expect some "three steps forward, two steps back" type progress. Celebrate every small step and think of creative ways to be supportive and encouraging when the participant faces challenges and feels discouraged.

express feelings of great discouragement or weariness — "I don't like my life the way it is now, but it is so hard to change it and I'm just too worn out." In this instance, the team may want to step back and take a modest break from its work. The team should ask how they can support the participant through this particular time and then check in again with the participant in two to three weeks to see how things are going. If the participant's motivation level is still very low, then the team members should suggest a face-to-face meeting to decide whether the working relationship should continue at this time.

In other instances, the participant may not be willing to do whatever is necessary for her self-improvement. At this point, the old cliché comes true: "It's hard to help those who aren't willing to help themselves." If a participant misses three meetings without offering a legitimate excuse, the team should communicate clearly that it is willing to continue the working relationship, but that the participant needs to prove with his or her actions a true commitment to that working relationship. If a conversation between the team members and the participant does not produce constructive change, the team may want to ask the start-up committee (or the program director) to step in and speak with the participant. Also, the team may want to contact the participant's caseworker, to see whether he or she has any insight on how to motivate or exhort the participant. If contacts by these individuals do not help to resolve the situation, the team may have to accept that there is no choice but to sever the relationship.

> ## Demolishing Stereotypes
>
> "Being a mentor has broken up my stereotypes of welfare recipients. It's easy to form a we/they attitude. Getting to know these women personally has made me re-evaluate my stereotypes. I understand now on a deeper level where they've come from. I know they really want to change, and watching them change has increased my hope."
>
> — B.B., a mentor involved in Mississippi's Faith and Families program

STEP 9: ENDING A MENTORING RELATIONSHIP

Conducting a Pre-exit Interview

Near the end of any mentoring relationship, the team, the participant, and the start-up committee (or program director, if the church chooses to have one) should complete a "pre-exit" interview. At this meeting (usually about one month before the end of the "formal" time commitment the team has made), the team and the participant review their original covenant and action plan and assess the progress made together. They can also identify the priority tasks to complete within the final month of the working relationship. If things have been going well, and both the team and the participant feel they would benefit from working together further, then they can draw up a new action plan for an extension of their work — for example, a commitment to work together for three more months. While it is possible that team members and the participant may end up having a friendship that will continue well beyond the extension of time agreed to, it is a good idea to set up formal parameters (e.g., work together three more months and then have another assessment/evaluation time) rather than leaving it indefinite.

Conducting an Exit Interview

At the conclusion of the formal relationship, the start-up committee or program director should complete exit interviews, separately, with the team and with the participant. In these interviews, the committee or program director asks the team members to evaluate their experience in the mentoring program. Similarly, the committee or program director interviews the participant to learn what was most helpful, and what was not helpful, about working with the team. This feedback from the teams and the participants can then serve as the basis for making improvements to the overall mentoring program. Listening to the team's experience can improve the mentor training process, for example. Perhaps one team successfully worked through some rocky times with its participant. That experience should be "documented" in a form that can help future mentor teams deal with problems they may encounter. And by listening to the participant, the church demonstrates that it values his or her input and believes that his or her comments can help future participants to flourish in the mentoring program. By incorporating these assessments, the mentoring program can be continually improved.

Involuntarily Ending a Mentoring Relationship

If it appears that the relationship is going to be involuntarily severed, the team should make every effort to have face-to-face closure with the participant. This allows the team to communicate its concern and care for the participant and its disappointment that things did not work out. In the absence of a face-to-face meeting, the team may want to write a letter to the participant, reaffirming their love and concern for him or her and highlighting any good experiences they had in working with him or her.

STEP 10: EVALUATION OF THE MENTORING MINISTRY

Defining Success

The church should define "success" broadly enough to include not only progress in job-specific areas (completing a résumé, securing a new job), but also overall progress (educational, family, spiritual, relational). Clearly the mentor team needs to focus on the concrete specifics of improving the participant's economic self-reliance through stable employment. But individuals are more than merely workers — they are mothers and fathers, daughters and sons, sisters and brothers, uncles and aunts, and friends. As Christians, our ministry should be flexible enough to provide help in areas that are not economic, but that will usually have some kind of impact on the family's economic life. The woman in an abusive relationship, for example, may secure a job but not improve her (or her children's) quality of life because the boyfriend drinks the paycheck away. The mother whose teenager is constantly in trouble in school may lose her new job because of the multiple times she must leave work to deal with her delinquent son.

Conducting Process and Results Oriented Evaluation

Evaluation must be both process- and results-oriented. Process-oriented evaluation is ongoing and determines whether or not goals are being achieved. Once a goal has been set, it should be evaluated within the first 30 days and modified if necessary. Remember, the relational team is committed to working together for one year, and you will want to check progress regularly in order to help the family reach the goal of self-sufficiency within that period of time. If there is no progress, change the goal or the action steps.

This form of evaluation includes asking the participant family how they think things are going and if they would like to do anything differently. It also includes celebrating successes, such as completing job training, finding employment, living within a budget for two months in a row, children's getting good grades in school, or children's completing all of their chores. These are major milestones to becoming self-sufficient and should be recognized and applauded by the entire team.

Results-oriented evaluation looks backwards and evaluates whether or not the ministry changed lives and met the established long-term goals. The long-term goals can be divided into different segments (i.e. job training, job placement, job retention) with the ultimate goal being self-sufficiency. Self-sufficiency must not be the only long-term goal, however. The ministry must be evaluated as to whether or not all involved have come to a fuller relationship with Jesus Christ through their work with one another. *Successful Christ-centered relational ministry is always mutually transformational.*

Chapter Five

LEARNING WHAT WORKS IN CHURCH-BASED MENTORING

LESSON 1: *"Connected" mentoring programs tend to be more successful than (unstructured) "autonomous" mentoring programs.*

In "connected" mentoring programs, the church provides a mentor team that walks with a welfare recipient who is engaged in some sort of structured "self-improvement" program offered by an entity outside the church. The "self-improvement program" might be a job training class sponsored by the Salvation Army, or a life skills class conducted by the local department of social services. "Autonomous" mentoring occurs when a church is linked with a welfare recipient who is not engaged in such a structured program. This can leave the mentoring relationship nebulous and unfocused, causing unease for both the mentors and participants (because the relationship is awkward and neither knows what they're supposed to be doing together). Autonomous mentoring can work if the church designs its own structure — insisting on regular face-to-face meetings, completing an "action plan" with the recipient that outlines goals and deadlines, holding its own job or life skills training classes, and so on. Structure in the relationship is critical: (a) It builds in greater accountability; (b) the participant's engagement in a "self-help program" indicates that he or she is serious about gaining independence from welfare, and therefore will be a more highly motivated person to mentor; (c) the structure provides definition to the mentor-participant relationship — it is a friendship, but it is a directed, purposeful friendship aiming toward specific goals (e.g., the participant's successful graduation from the self-help program, the participant's successful completion of a personal financial plan or a personal strategic plan); and (d) structured mentoring programs are more volunteer-friendly because the mentors are more clear on what their role is. They are less likely to believe they have to "do everything" for the recipient and feel totally overwhelmed. Also, the friendship between the mentor and the participant is almost always a little awkward at first, because the two are strangers and perhaps rather different. The fact that there is a structured program in which the participant is engaged gives the relationship something concrete around which to form and grow.

LESSON 2: *Accurate diagnosis is critical.*

It's very important for the mentor team and the participant to examine together the *root causes* of the recipient's financial challenges. Recipients who cannot manage their money well will continue to face difficulties even if the mentoring program helps them to find better-paying employment. Similarly, a program that provides recipients with affordable day care and transportation will not truly help recipients who lack the respectful attitude and reliability necessary for retaining employment. And a program that offers terrific personal support and counseling, but fails to equip the recipient with the basic job skills necessary for securing stable employment, may also prove insufficient. Effective programs make an accurate diagnosis of the principal reasons why a needy family is in need and then tailor their assistance accordingly.

LESSON 3: *Mentors and participants should sign a covenant at the beginning of their working relationship.*

The covenant outlines the commitment each is making to the other, and clearly defines the roles and expectations of each. From the beginning of the relationship, the participants and the mentors must understand what is expected of them. The participants need to understand what they can, and cannot, ask the mentors for. The mentors need to know what they are committing themselves to do, and then be faithful to do it. A subsidiary of this lesson is the importance of clearly spelling out what role, if any, financial benevolence will play in the mentoring program.

LESSON 4: *A personal action plan will help guide the participants and their mentors.*

An action plan is a strategy document designed by the participants and their mentors that outlines goals and steps for accomplishing those goals. The action plan includes a timeline and deadlines for the accomplishment of various goals.

A subsidiary of this lesson is that *regular, structured, face-to-face contact with the program participant is essential.*

LESSON 5: *Effective mentoring almost always involves time-intensive, personalized help.*

This lesson has at least three implications. First, be straightforward with your volunteers that this ministry is going to take time. Second, utilize mentor *teams* rather than merely relying on a one-on-one model. This both precludes volunteer burnout and allows mentors to work in pairs (which can be important, for example, when babysitting the participant's kids). Third, put someone on every mentor team who has daytime availability. It might be a homemaker, a retired person, or a self-employed person with a flexible schedule. Typically, mentoring will involve helping the participant with personal business matters — such as dealing with the IRS, the DMV, or other government agencies — that can only be attended to from 9 to 5 Monday through Friday.

LESSON 6: *The mentors must be willing to pry a little, and the participants must be willing to build a transparent relationship with the mentors.*

This is, obviously, one of the most difficult parts of the mentoring relationship. But asking tough questions is necessary, holding people accountable is necessary, and getting the participant to "talk straight" is necessary. In a nutshell, sometimes "tough love" is necessary.

LESSON 7: *Set a minimum of six months for the relationship.*

The first 30 to 90 days are typically spent in a "crisis management" phase. This phase involves frequent meetings and focuses on the participant's most immediate obstacles to self-sufficiency (finding day care, clearing up back bills, re-establishing telephone service, obtaining car repairs, setting up a budget, and identifying employment opportunities). Participants tend to be understandably shy about revealing all the problems that need attention. As friendship with the volunteers grows deeper, however, the participants open up more. This may mean that the mentor team will not even learn of some significant problems until four to five months into the relationship. Consequently, an additional several months of working together is preferable.

LESSON 8: *Pre-exit interviews are a useful guide to the participants in making the transition out of the mentoring program.*

Some mentoring programs utilize pre-exit interviews when there are two months remaining in the formal mentoring relationship. At these sessions, the mentors and participants review the progress they've made together and assess what remains to be done to help the participant meet the goals identified in his or her action plan. This allows everyone to have a sense of where they need to go in the final couple of months. It also can help to encourage mentors to stay involved with the participant even beyond the "formal" mentoring time, if the mentors feel that there is more that they can do to assist the participant.

"We've Become Real Good Friends"

"To know Maria is to love her. She feels like I'm a mother figure — that's what she has said. Mainly I see myself as an encourager. We've become real good friends. When I met Maria, she had come through a nervous breakdown, had really been struggling emotionally, and I had been too, so that was an instant bond. We've been able to encourage each other emotionally because we've had some shared experiences there. We really enjoy talking. She's real open with me [about spiritual things]. That's another way I encourage her."

— J.T., church mentor in Michigan who has worked with Maria, a 27-year-old Hispanic mother of four, for several months

LESSON 9: *Make sure the church carries an insurance policy that provides liability protection for the volunteers involved in its mentoring program, including coverage dealing with an at-fault car accident involving the volunteer's automobile.*

This is a rather mundane issue, but it is an important one, as it will increase the volunteers' comfort level in providing transportation help to participants.

LESSON 10: *Intentionally support volunteers.*

The mentors need to be trained, encouraged, prayed for, and appreciated. Training should cover, at a minimum, such topics as relating cross-culturally; developing active listening, goal-setting, and problem-solving skills; assessing the program participant's needs and assets; learning how to set appropriate boundaries; understanding typical participant problems; and learning how to winsomely present the reality of your faith. To provide ongoing learning and encouragement, several welfare-to-work mentoring programs I've visited conduct occasional meetings in which various volunteer mentoring teams gather together to swap stories, compare experiences, problem-solve, and pray for each another. Volunteers I interviewed were uniformly fervent in their praise for such gatherings. New teams felt they gained from the wisdom and trial-and-error experience of mentor teams that had already completed some mentoring assignments. Additionally, by meeting other teams, volunteers were able to expand their network of contacts further.

Appendix A[2]

TIPS FOR RECRUITING AND ENCOURAGING VOLUNTEERS

TIP 1:
Know your mission and put it in writing, so volunteers can clearly understand it. (A person has to know and understand the vision in order to "catch" it!)

TIP 2:
Know what kind of people you are looking for. List the types of skills, interests, passions, life experiences, resources, and spiritual gifts you believe would be helpful to your ministry.

TIP 3:
Write out "job descriptions" for the various volunteer positions open in your ministry. Share these with interested individuals and post them on the church's community bulletin board.

TIP 4:
Educate volunteers by describing profiles of "typical" program participants. If you are partnering with a nonprofit agency or the department of social services, have one of its staff members come to the recruitment/orientation meetings to talk about the potential program participants and their needs.

TIP 5:
Excite and inspire volunteers by sharing testimonies about "success stories" from your (and

[2] Most of this material is drawn from a 1997 workshop at the Christian Development Conference by Yvonne Dodd, former executive director of Hope for New York.

others') church-based ministries.[3] If possible, have experienced volunteers from similar ministries in other churches on hand to talk about their experiences and answer questions that new or potential volunteers may have about what's involved in being an effective volunteer.

TIP 6:

Clearly define the ministry's expectations (time commitment, role, responsibilities).

TIP 7:

Appreciate your volunteers! Hold an annual Volunteer Appreciation Banquet, highlight volunteers teams and their work in the church's newsletter, send thank-you notes, give out certificates of achievement, and so on.

TIP 8:

Solicit volunteer input. "Exit interviews" conducted with volunteers at the end of a ministry season are effective for soliciting volunteers' suggestions and constructive criticisms. You can also have volunteers complete a survey questionnaire that asks for suggestions for improvement.

TIP 9:

Communicate regularly with your volunteers — never let them feel they have been forgotten! You may even want to create a special publication/newsletter for your volunteers.

TIP 10:

Celebrate success. Give the volunteers opportunities to testify about how God worked in their lives through their service experiences. Have volunteers share these testimonies before adult Sunday school classes or in a worship service. Or ask them to write up their testimony for church publications. This both affirms volunteers and communicates vision to the rest of the congregation, thus stimulating greater interest in, and support of, the church's outreach ministries.

---

[3] Several such stories are recorded in the following articles by Amy L. Sherman: "Little Miracles: How Churches are Responding to Welfare Reform," *The American Enterprise* (Jan.-Feb. 1998); "Thy Neighbor's Keeper," *Reason* (Aug.-Sep. 1996); "A New Path Out of Poverty? A Close Look at Mississippi's Faith and Family Program," *The American Enterprise* (July-Aug. 1996); "A Measure of Our Greatness," *Rutherford* (November 1996); and "STEPping Out on Faith – And Off Welfare," *Christianity Today* (June 17, 1996).

Appendix B

KEYS TO COLLABORATION BETWEEN CHURCHES AND LOCAL GOVERNMENT

KEY 1: "Ground-floor-up" involvement

Churches must be partners, not subcontractors, with government. That means the church must be permitted to participate in the design of new initiatives from the beginning.

KEY 2: Sympathy and respect

Government officials must eschew the elitist perspective that only highly educated professionals are equipped to help poor people. They should acknowledge that lay volunteers can provide crucial emotional support and moral guidance to needy families — things that government, by its nature, cannot offer. The government partner must allow religious groups the flexibility and creativity to meet the family's needs — even when ministries rely on strategies remarkably different from those employed by government agencies.

KEY 3: Discerning teachability

Churches should respect their government partners and recognize that caseworkers have valuable experience and practical wisdom from which the churches can learn. Nonetheless, churches must be discerning, since their presuppositions may differ substantially from those of their secular partners.

KEY 4: Connected autonomy

In most current church-state partnerships, the church is willing to do a lot but doesn't want full responsibility for the disadvantaged families it is assisting. Churches want assurances that the individuals they serve will also be linked to government-sponsored programs that address needs the churches themselves cannot meet. At the same time, churches want to help poor people without excessive governmental interference that might squelch the spiritual character of their outreach. Churches want, in short, "connected autonomy." That is, they want to be a part of a team that surrounds the needy family — a team on which they play a significant, largely unfettered, and unique role, but a team nonetheless.

Appendix C[4]

MOVING TOWARD RELATIONAL MINISTRY – THE NEW FOCUS MODEL

Probably 75 percent of the church secretaries in America have at least once received a telephone call from a stranger asking for the church's financial assistance. The Bible makes clear that the Church is responsible for helping the needy; the tricky part is discerning what kind of help is truly helpful. Many churches offer emergency financial aid, clothing, and groceries to lower-income families. These kinds of "relief" assistance are often very useful and appropriate. But, as discussed earlier in this guide, "relief" can be inadequate — or irrelevant — for certain families. Able-bodied poor people often need "developmental" assistance, not mere relief aid. Developmental aid is aimed at addressing the underlying causes of the individual's financial distress. Most churches desire that their help truly help, rather than merely providing a temporary solution. So many churches ask, "How can we make the shift from commodity-based 'relief' assistance only to a relational, developmental outreach ministry?" New Focus, a Christ-centered ministry in Michigan, can help with such a shift.

Let's suppose Sandy calls a church utilizing the New Focus system and asks for $200. She needs the money to pay an electricity bill; she doesn't have the funds herself and fears her service will be turned off. As the phone counselor who answered Sandy's call continues the conversation, she learns that Sandy frequently runs short of cash to pay her utility bills. Based on what Sandy reports concerning her income from part-time work, food stamps, and housing assistance, it seems that Sandy should be able to meet her monthly financial obligations. So, the phone counselor lets Sandy know that the church might be willing to help her with this specific need, if Sandy is willing to adopt a plan for managing her finances that will help her to avoid this situation in the future. If Sandy is interested, she can attend a New Focus introductory meeting at the church on Wednesday night, and she'll receive a free bag of gro-

---

[4] Most of the information in this appendix is taken from New Focus. They can be reached at (616)895-5356 or at 6837 Lake Michigan Drive, P.O. Box 351, Allendale, MI 49401. See Chapter 8 in *The Welfare of My Neighbor* for more information.

ceries just for showing up. In addition, the phone volunteer lets Sandy know that the church provides free child care during the New Focus meeting and that refreshments will be served. The volunteer also informs Sandy that if, after attending the meeting, she decides that she wants to join New Focus and get some help in taking positive steps toward change, then trained church volunteers will meet with her to design an action plan and figure out the ways in which the church can help.

So Sandy and her kids go the New Focus-affiliated church on Wednesday night for the introductory meeting. Her children join the other kids for a time of crafts, singing, Bible lessons, and games. Sandy and the other adults hear a presentation about the New Focus system. The church offers no-interest loans, small financial gifts, other material resources (food, clothing, household items), and services (budget counseling, prayer support, transportation) to individuals who become members of New Focus. Members, in turn, agree to attend weekly meetings with a personal financial coach who helps them establish a workable spending plan. The financial coach may hold the member's checkbook and credit cards if compulsive spending is a problem. Otherwise, the member keeps the checkbook but writes his or her checks once a week during the budget counseling session. Counselors and members discuss the small steps members can take to get back on their feet financially and eventually to become debt-free.

If Sandy makes a commitment to become a New Focus member and attend the weekly class, the New Focus director will complete an "intake" with her. (An intake is a form on which basic information about Sandy — age, family size, address, phone number, occupation, sources of income, fixed monthly expenditures, availability of relatives or friends nearby who can help, church affiliation if any, and so on — is recorded.) Or, the church may use an existing intake already completed by staff at the agency that referred Sandy to the church. After completing the intake, the New Focus director converses with Sandy about what her immediate needs are and what areas of her life she would like to change. Then the director, a financial coach, and a deacon involved with the New Focus program meet with Sandy in her home to begin designing together a strategic, long-term plan for helping Sandy to exit the welfare system or otherwise achieve greater economic self-sufficiency. Sandy then begins attending the weekly "Steps to Change" class at the church. By the time she completes this six-week course, Sandy will have made a list of her top spending priorities in a "Spending Plan Book." She will also have had the opportunity to complete a "self-assessment" by using a unique tool called the "Heart House" booklet. The Heart House booklet allows New Focus members to evaluate themselves, assess what's going right and what's going wrong in their lives, what their needs and assets are, what goals they wish to pursue, and the changes they might need to make to accomplish those goals. Sandy can go through the Heart House booklet privately, which allows her to do some genuine soul-searching. Then, once the booklet is completed, Sandy can share it with her financial coach or other New Focus helpers, and they will be able to get a better idea of what Sandy thinks about herself — and what the main changes are that she wants to make. Equipped with this knowledge, the financial coach and other New Focus volunteers are better positioned both to encourage Sandy and to assist her in making good choices that accord with the goals and priorities she has set for herself. This allows the New Focus volunteers to offer different kinds of choices to Sandy rather than making the choices for her.

The work Sandy and the New Focus volunteers do together are guided by the goals Sandy

More on New Focus

New Focus's comprehensive strategy for effectively targeting the use of church benevolence funds embodies sound biblical principles concerning responsible compassion. Churches adopting the New Focus program must commit a specific percentage of their benevolence funds to the program, including money to pay a part-time New Focus director at their own church. (Churches are, of course, free to find out whether there is a church member willing to serve in this position without a salary.) New Focus trains the church director on how to establish an incentive-based budget counseling program and mobilize the laity for involvement in "Compassion Circles" that befriend and mentor individuals participating in the weekly New Focus program. Participating churches agree to make space available in their own buildings for the weekly evening meeting and for a "store" at which New Focus members can redeem earned vouchers for clothing and food. New Focus calls itself a "change management system," since it seeks to help people in financial trouble to take small, consistent steps toward positive change. Its core is the biblically based budget counseling program, but New Focus is about much more than just money management.

New Focus's model is relational, aims at long-term change, and builds in accountability. New Focus's approach is also volunteer-friendly. Individuals are more likely to be willing to help Sandy when they understand that they are part of a whole team surrounding her. Also, each friend in the Compassion Circle makes only a twice-per-month time commitment. Financial coaches make a more significant commitment — a weekly meeting. Financial coaches, however, benefit from the fact that their coaching is reinforced by the weekly general teaching session and by the incentive/rewards system built into New Focus' program. Churches involved in the New Focus program benefit because their benevolence funds now are tied to a variety of other supports (Bible-based teaching, budget counseling, emotional support, and other practical helps) that help address the root problems underlying a person's immediate cash emergency. Moreover, church money is going to help individuals whom church members are getting to know personally.

Even more importantly, the New Focus program is evangelistic, overtly encouraging members to follow God's will in dealing with their money, their families, their work, and their problems. While a member need not be a Christian to join the program, he or she is told up front that the Bible is the program's main textbook.

New Focus members benefit from the ministry because in addition to financial aid, they are given emotional support and taught the skills they need to live healthier, balanced, responsible lives. Often, people are dissatisfied with their current lifestyles, but feel that they lack the strength to take the steps necessary to improve their lives. New Focus provides them a network of caring support and tangible incentives for taking those steps.

has outlined — goals related to such issues as her family relationships, her education, her career, and her housing situation. With everyone "on the same page" about where Sandy is and where she wants to be, the New Focus helpers are able to encourage her and celebrate with her as she makes progress towards her goals. Basically, the New Focus volunteers encourage Sandy to envision a better, healthier future for herself and her family, and then help her to identify the steps she needs to take to get there.

As a New Focus member, Sandy and her kids will attend the New Focus meetings once a week. Each meeting consists of two sessions. During the first session, Sandy will meet individually with her financial coach. Each week, Sandy determines three small steps that she can take to move her toward her long-range goals. She and the coach review her progress. As Sandy accomplishes the various steps, she will be rewarded with various incentives provided by the church: laundry soap, discounted goods, groceries. Sandy can also let her financial coach know of any specific needs she has, such as car repairs or a winter coat. The coach then writes these requests on small pieces of paper resembling apples and hangs them on the church's "Giving Tree." (The Tree is placed in a public area in the church building where church members can look over the various requests and see whether they can provide any of the goods or services needed.) During the second session, Sandy and other members will participate in a small group discussion on "Steps to Financial Freedom," a Bible-based budgeting curriculum. The small group will also hold a "prayer and share" time together and fellowship around a light meal.

After Sandy graduates from the six-week "Steps to Change" class, she is included in a "Compassion Circle" that will support her as she continues to take small steps to positive change. (Members of Sandy's Circle will likely have already attended her graduation ceremony and celebrated her completion of the first phase of the New Focus program with her.) The Circle is a small group of individuals or couples from the church who will meet regularly with Sandy to cheer her progress. New Focus recruits volunteers interested in being in a Circle and asks them to identify what their ministry passions are, and what unique life experiences and/or educational experiences they can draw from. Some volunteers may want to help a single mom; others may want to help an unemployed man; others may have a burden for the low-income elderly; still others may feel they could best be used to mentor a young mother. The Circle members will already have met together several times, on a twice-monthly basis, before they meet Sandy. This allows them to get to know each other and build a sense of "team." They will have also each completed a "Heart House" assessment, which helps them to look carefully at their own lives and see where God's faithfulness and power has been evident in the past. The Circle members will also discuss together their personal testimonies and their convictions about how to serve others, how to achieve family harmony, how to respect authority and be authority, how to forgive others, and other crucial issues.

Let's say that a Circle that had requested to work with single moms is the one chosen to be matched with Sandy. Sandy and her Circle will then start meeting twice per month for at least a year; during this time, Sandy also continues meeting weekly with her financial coach. Once a month, Circle members will help each other complete a service project: One month they might repaint Sandy's apartment, another month they might resurface another member's driveway. This way, people who have difficulty receiving become receivers and givers, and people who have difficulty giving become givers and receivers.

Appendix D

URBAN-SUBURBAN CHURCH PARTNERSHIPS – LESSONS FROM A CHURCH LEADER

By Laurie Carter

S cott Oostdyk is no stranger to the issue of urban-suburban partnerships, being the son of Harv Oostdyk, who blazed new trails in America's urban arena throughout the 1960s-80s (see poem pages 136-137 in *The Welfare of My Neighbor*). Scott, a law partner at McGuire, Woods, Battle and Boothe, was appointed to head Virginia's welfare reform efforts as deputy secretary of health and human resources from May of 1996 to November of 1997. Scott has been active in Richmond's STEP (Strategies to Elevate People) ministry for several years, part of that time as chairman of the board. Scott firmly believes that "the way to build back a successful inner city is to build back the institutions that help people learn values and the right skills necessary to work in a market economy." He brings a wealth of insight and experience to bear both on the Church's role in the city and on developing effective urban-suburban partnerships.

Q. *From your own experiences working with suburban and urban churches, how do you nurture the idea of real partnership in the city and not simply bolster the typical, one-directional mindset that says, "Let's just go in there and help those poor people?"*

A. In my experience, things work best when you come up with a plan to work on defined targeted areas, and then concentrate on them over a long period of time. The big antidote to the kind of paternalism you're talking about is taking a long-term view of the problem. Things weren't created overnight and they don't get fixed overnight. A suburban church might find a church partner in a particular urban neighborhood, and then just simply bond at the level of saying, "Let's make a long-term commitment to the work that you do. What work do you have? What are your dreams and visions for your neighborhood?" Start by helping them accomplish some of those. But the reality is that people in the suburban church may be more trained in their careers, more experienced, have more contacts and more resources. So don't be foolish about the fact that after working on their agenda for a little while you'll want to look at things from the perspective of what the suburban church has to offer too. The key is to have both an institutional approach — which addresses the basic problems that derail people and how you go about fixing them over time — and a personal approach, which says, "Let's give something of our life in a way that allows us to be friends with you," because the best program is friendship, just like the best social program is a job. And you keep that front and center.

The key is to have a strategy. I've seen totally divergent strategies, from all over the country, that work well, and the common denominator is always commitment. You can't accomplish anything by coming in with what Francis Schaeffer used to call "triumphalism" — the idea that it's more fun to mobilize against the problem then it is to solve it. And evangelicals are particularly guilty of that. We love in time of crisis to declare war on something, but we're usually not around for the victory. So I believe that if you have one or two people with vision, they can usually sustain the church's transition into this type of partnership.

Q. *You assert that the key to successful suburban partnership in the city is strategy. For suburban churches interested in getting involved in urban ministry, but that aren't sure how to go about it, describe some effective partnerships you've seen and what has made them effective.*

A. First of all, there's no magic plan. So I hesitate to say that anything that I could offer would be, "Wow, this is the best way to do it," because the best way is commitment. Why? If you said, "I'm going to start the biggest church in the history of the world," I just don't think you would do it the way Jesus did it. You wouldn't pick 12 backwoods people and say, "I'm just going to be with you for three years and then I'm going to leave you totally alone." That's no plan. That's not a church. We "know better" now. But yet that's the way the Church of Christ was started, so obviously what he did was pick people who would provide total commitment. He didn't pick the people capable of providing the best plans. Peter was not the best diplomat. They were simply committed people, and Jesus knew that commitment would outstrip a lot of ability much of the time.

I had a minister come to me once and tell me that the son of the assistant rector of his church had been shot (he was a suburban kid working in a suburban store and he got shot by a robber). The church was very distressed, and now murder was enemy number one because it had touched their church. But there had been murders going on in our city forever, just in other parts of town. Yet he said he wanted to start a rally against crime, going into the toughest crime neighborhoods, and just declare war on it. My response to him was, "What in the world makes you think that, just because you're mad now, all of a sudden you can go lead something where other people have endured this pain a whole lot longer than you?

Instead of going in there and being a leader, why don't you go in there for a little while and be a follower — to the people and the ministers who have marched against this problem in their [high-]crime neighborhoods for a long time?" You see, what I didn't want to scare away was this man's tremendous resource and his pain, but I wanted to keep him from failing. So I think that the best thing that people can do is start small. Start with individual efforts, working with people who are already committed to the problem. When we started STEP, the first thing we did was go and find urban pastors who were struggling with few resources, big dreams and big commitment. And we said, "Let our church simply help your church and learn from you about what you're doing, but in time it will be a two-way street." From that grew a lot of programming and the ability to involve a lot of people.

So to be real practical, the *first principle* in any program development is *listen* to the people who have experience in your chosen neighborhood with attacking the problems of that neighborhood. Then the *second principle* would be *think* about root causes and desired outcomes. Once you've had time to evaluate why a neighborhood is the way it is, then sit down and start looking at root causes. In Gilpin Court, the housing project we've worked in for 15 years, our assessment of root causes was that welfare had stagnated the 786 families, and the kids were learning from the parents all the wrong strategies to succeed. The myth is that it is all spiritual, that if you just give people the right principles they will make the right choices. But that's not always true. Often times people need other structural supports that the church can't or doesn't provide until it commits to provide them. So the key is to trace the problem all the way back to its genesis and minister there. Don't just do "clothes closets" and "Thanksgiving turkeys." Do I think there is a place for these? Yes, I call them mercy ministries and I think they help humanize your efforts, because, frankly, immediate need is something that Jesus worked on all the time. He did it so that people could hear him and accept him for his heart of teaching. But you are deluded if you think that all the Church has to do is show up every Thanksgiving for two days and then disappear until next Thanksgiving.

Then the *third principle* would be *abide.* After you have discovered your root causes and planned your desired outcomes, then you just have to hang in there and be faithful. The only way that churches can do effective social work is by being faithful. One thing that eases our work in Gilpin Court is that we have been around for 15 years with no break in service. We are the most sustained church-based ministry, and therefore everybody knows our name. And the *fourth principle* would be *partner*, because partnering is really the way of the future. All charities are now being forced to partner; the day when you could work in isolation with just your own service model is over.

Finally, the *fifth principle* would be *promote.* Churches generally don't do well in sustaining a marketing plan. We do it with our stewardship — we are the best promoters of financial stewardship in the world. There are only a few stewardship verses in the whole Bible, but they get preached 81 times a year! And we make everybody aware that this is something that is going to happen across the whole church. But we don't do that when it comes to issues like poverty, which is mentioned more often than stewardship. We don't teach about our responsibility to respond to poverty. Some think we shouldn't, because it would be just a guilt message, not an empowering message, since we don't have the infrastructure and knowledge in the Church to know how to fight poverty. So the spiritual leaders of a church need to understand and come to grips with what the church's role is regarding "the least of these." It is clear in Scripture. When we encounter economic disparity the Bible tells us to be extra sensitive.

What form that takes is a matter of the leadership of the local assembly, but clearly there has to be a response, not just from the "bleeding hearts," but from everybody who wants to bear the label of *Christian*. Pastors need to preach about this at unexpected times, and also have people gifted in this area acknowledged as leaders and empowered by the church to be the head of a response — empowered to do it with the same vitality that the church would demonstrate in planning a new building. Ultimately, this is a leadership issue. So teach the Scripture in such a way that people can understand their responsibility, and create within the church the infrastructure (leadership, strategy and resources) for urban outreach. You can get 400 people to do anything with the right emphasis. But the question is how do you maintain 5, 6 or 10 emphases at the same time? This is where churches have a hard time. Every church has a top three — it's in their culture.

Elevating this type of outreach closer to the top three is a matter of making a strategy that is broad enough to pick up everyone's talents, having something for the banker to do as well as the retired person with 20 hours to invest.

Q. *You've described some steps or principles for churches who want to be involved in ministry in the city. What are some lessons learned or pieces of advice you would give to churches as they begin or continue on the road to partnership?*

A. The *first lesson* I've learned is to *celebrate every small accomplishment*, because that feeds the sense of purpose and hope that we all need to stay involved. But realize that your true accomplishment will be a long way away if you are starting off fresh in a brand new partnership. You have to have a sense that one child who got an "A" on a report card instead of a "C" could be the cause for a church-wide celebration, if that's all you got. In the front page of the Metro section of our newspaper today, there is an article about a woman who came through our Jobs Partnership program who had lost a $50,000 job because of downsizing. She fell into a deep depression and landed in a housing project with her two kids. Yet now she is building her life back. She says that our program and spiritual training is what gave her the spiritual hope to energize her physical skills. Without that healing to her spirit she wouldn't have been able to turn around and start a cleaning company, for which she is now hiring two other people. What is more, one of our partnering churches (ironically, the same church where I told the rector don't go in and have a crime march) went out and found her 15 customers from their church. They meet with her every other month in a friend's club to share a meal, encourage and pray for her. They haven't spent any money nor done anything more than just encourage her and be with her, but they have changed the woman's life. That's the kind of climate we're living in. You can do that. But you can't do that if you don't have vision for the small things and how important they are. But at the same time you plan to be involved with big things. Let God also use you in big things.

The *second lesson* learned is to *have patience with the cultivation of your leadership team.* Leadership is everything. I've developed a favorite slogan right now which says "great successes begin with good leadership." [Without leadership,] it is not clear who's going to help define [your objectives] or correct your course if you're off. So I think churches need to [get] it down to some form of a good church-based or neighborhood-based ministry model. And the quicker you get into organization, the better your chances of sustaining something. People come and go, your key volunteer will go. But if you have an organizational structure that replaces itself, then you can sustain.

The *third lesson* learned over the years is to *avoid fads*. Over 15 years in the work here, we've been through so many fads, like the anti-crime fad, the literacy fad, the drug fad, and now we just finished with the welfare fad. But all these are just different societal interpretations of the same problem — human hopelessness, human disempowerment, and human potential. You must keep your program attuned to the immortal truths that people need Christ and equipping in their faith, but they also need to be able to read, to navigate the employment structures; they need contacts [with] stable business environments, upward mobility, solid housing and good schools. They need all of it. The only answer that is satisfying, and truly honoring to God, is doing everything. But you can't do everything on your first day. We need to be better about taking the fixed truths of the Scriptures and finding ways of making them very palatable and very appealing in a poverty environment.

Q. *Any other advice for churches about partnering in the city?*

A. For churches that have had nominal involvement or have had mercy ministries only — to those I would say, pick a quality partner carefully. Pick a church minister whom you have cross-referenced or somebody who has a viable inner city work already going on. Don't start your own; go to someone who already has one that you admire, bring a small team and just abide with those folks. Learn about what they are doing and how they could utilize help. They may not even have a vision for it, because most urban ministries are survivalist, going day to day to meet their needs and those around them, not always thinking long term/big picture. You can avoid a lot of mistakes if you go in on the agenda of people who are already in the community.

But to the ministries that are already involved — to them I would say to whom much is given, much is required. If you have been given the gift of access in a community, if you have been given a gift of presence, then you may have an obligation of leadership. So you may have to stand up and offer to have additional churches come and meet with you to explore whether or not your ministry can become some sort of a focal point for their efforts, and whether or not your expansion plan might include some of their vision too. For example, although we (STEP) have 15 years of experience with what we do and have enough name recognition to continue to receive resources in order to do more, we still have a leadership obligation. At our board retreat in January we're going to sit down and figure out which other ministries around us we may have an obligation to partner with.

STEP in Richmond started because a bunch of people from Richmond went separately to a conference in Washington, D.C. where Pastor E.V. Hill (who was president of STEP in the early 1980s) stood up to give a teaching. Afterwards, a man raised his hand and said, "I'd like to apply what I've learned here back in my own city. But I don't know anyone there to get started with who is in the inner city" (he represented a suburban group). Pastor Hill responded by saying, "Well, is anyone else here from Richmond?" And lo and behold, on the other side of the room was a bunch of people from an urban church. And they said, "Well, we're from a city church." So Pastor Hill said, "Well, I'm going to marry you. By the powers vested in me I now pronounce you partners. Go back to your city and minister together." And that in fact is what happened. Those two groups came, having been joined together in that meeting, and built the basis of what is now the STEP ministry. Two groups of people, coming together at a conference, and for 15 years those same people have been walking together, building this ministry that now touches thousands of people. (For more information on STEP Richmond, see Chapter 8 of *The Welfare of My Neighbor.*)

Laurie Carter serves on the Urban Outreach team of The Falls Church (Episcopal) in Falls Church, Va., and holds a Masters of Divinity degree, with an emphasis on international and urban missions, from Gordon-Conwell Theological Seminary.

Appendix E[5]

CASE STUDY – PROBLEM SOLVING WITH WELFARE FAMILIES

When problem solving, it is well to remember that a participant may view problems quite differently from the church volunteers. Try to put yourself in the participant's shoes. Daily problems facing a needy person could overwhelm anyone. Imagine this scenario:

The alarm goes off at 5 a.m. Mary Smith drags herself out of bed and into a cold shower (the water heater is broken). She has no breakfast — there is just enough cereal to feed the children. She awakens the eight-year-old, who must stay home by himself for two hours and then walk to the school bus stop. Mary takes the four-year-old with her on the bus to drop her off at day care. The little girl sneezes, and Mary fervently hopes the child is not coming down with a cold (or worse) because she will lose her job if she misses another day of work to stay home with a sick child. One hour and three bus transfers later, Mary, already weary, arrives at work. After she waits tables for four hours, the boss sends her home because there aren't enough customers to justify working a full shift. Mary picks up her daughter at day care and then stops by the welfare office to see a caseworker, waiting for two hours with a cranky child who has had no nap. On the way home, Mary gets off the bus at the store to buy groceries and cigarettes with the $8 she earned in tips today. Now, with no bus fare left, she walks half a mile lugging the

---

[5] Reprinted by permission of the Evergreen Freedom Foundation (with minor alterations). The case study comes from the Foundation's "Church Training Manual" for the Faith-Based Welfare Reform Project in Washington state. The Project mobilizes and trains churches to mentor families going from welfare to work. For more information, contact Priscilla Martens, Project Coordinator, at (360) 956-3482.

bag of groceries in one arm and the still cranky child in the other. When she gets home, the eight-year-old is waiting outside. He got sick at school, but since Mary had already left work when the school called, they sent him home with a volunteer. She puts together a few things for dinner and then walks to the Laundromat to do three loads of laundry. The children stay at home by themselves. At 9 p.m., she tucks the children into bed, falls into bed herself soon after, and cries herself to sleep.

It's hard for most of us to imagine how someone could live this way for one day, much less for days on end. This mother has financial needs, child-care needs, lack of transportation, nobody to turn to for help in a crisis, unbearable stress, and hopelessness. How can a team of volunteers sort through all these problems and help this mother create a self-sufficient life?

PROBLEM SOLVING

As the volunteer team talks with Mary, they realize she has come to a breaking point. How can the volunteers best help her? The problem-solving process includes the following steps.

1. ***State what appears to be the problem.*** This is the problem as presented by the participant, but it can be changed later based on additional information and analysis. *Example:* Mary says, "Life is no longer worth living." The volunteer team responds, "Frustrating things are happening in your life that cause you to feel this way."

2. ***Gather facts.*** What happened? What were the circumstances? Who is affected? Is the problem likely to happen again? *Example:* A volunteer says to Mary, "Tell us more about what's happening in your life." Mary then proceeds to tell the team about the horrible day she experienced.

3. ***Restate the problem.*** Based on additional information, the problem may not be exactly the same as was originally stated. But be sure that the participant is in agreement about the problem before going on to the next steps. *Example:* "All of the following (list items) happened to you in one day, and you would like to gain more control over your life. But we can't work on all of these problems at once. What is the most important thing that you would like to work on first?" Mary responds, "I don't have a decent job that will support my family." The team has helped Mary identify a specific, manageable problem that they can now work on and solve together.

4. ***Identify some possible solutions.*** This is the time for brainstorming which involves spontaneous, free thinking. It may seem childlike, but don't critique or evaluate ideas at this point — just let them flow! *Example:* A volunteer says to Mary, "What would you consider the ideal job?" For the next 20 minutes, the team and Mary discuss job possibilities based on what she really enjoys doing.

5. ***Evaluate alternatives.*** Now you can weed out ideas and select those that are most workable. Remember, alternatives must be workable from the participant's point of view, not the volunteer team's.

Example: Mary enjoys working with her hands and is an excellent typist. She would like to do computer data entry but has no computer skills.

The team is now ready to plan solutions and set goals.

GOAL SETTING

A goal is a statement of results to be achieved. Goals describe (a) conditions that will exist when the desired outcome has been accomplished, and (b) a time frame in which the outcome is to be completed.

6. ***Goals answer three questions*** — who, what, and when. Goals can be measured and evaluated.

Example: Mary and the volunteers use a Goals/Action Steps form that lists goals and the action steps necessary to accomplish them. It specifies who is responsible for implementing them under a specific time frame. They write the first goal: Within the next eight months, Mary will have a full-time job doing computer data entry.

7. ***Implement the goal.*** This answers the "how" question by listing the action steps that must be taken in order to achieve the goal. Each person responsible for the action step is named as well as the expected completion date.

Example: Under Action Steps on the form, the team lists the following:

Person Responsible	Action Step	Date for Completion
Mary	Enroll in computer course at community college — two nights a week for six months	w/in one week
Mrs. Johnson (*volunteer, retired teacher*)	Babysit Mary's children two nights a week and tutor the eight-year-old in reading	every week for six months
Mr. and Mrs. Thomas (*volunteer couple*)	Help Mary develop a budget, plan menus, and take her grocery shopping once a week for one month	w/in one month
Mary	Ask neighbor who has nine-year-old boy if she can be available for emergency child-care assistance	w/in one week
Mr. Owens (*young single volunteer*)	Repair water heater	w/in one week

Note that these steps address some of Mary's problems but not all of them. She still has inadequate transportation and child care, but she now has a specific time frame in which she can expect things to get better. The volunteers offer some concrete forms of help (babysitting, budgeting, and home repair), but this assistance is time-limited and aimed at helping Mary achieve her goal of self-sufficiency. The volunteers do not offer cash or other "easy" solutions, but offer their time, talents, and personal involvement. The volunteers also do not have unrealistic expectations. Mary wants to quit smoking, but has never been able to do so. Even though none of the volunteers smoke, no one suggests that Mary try to quit smoking at this point in time. They believe it is far more important for her to work on her employment goal, and they will address the smoking issue at another time.

8. ***Evaluate the results.*** Did the goal achieve the desired results? If not, make the changes necessary to achieve the desired results.

Example: Mary tries to enroll in a computer course but finds that the course is full and that she will have to wait for one month. Mr. and Mrs. Thomas have an old computer and will set it up in Mary's home and teach her some fundamentals while she waits to enroll in the course.

CONFRONTING IN LOVE

Probably the most difficult part of relational ministry will be confrontation. No one likes to have to confront another, but sometimes it is necessary for change and growth. Ignoring problems and hoping they will go away may result in the participant not achieving self-sufficiency. But confrontation should never be done in an impulsive, demeaning manner. Be thoroughly prepared before confronting, and consider these guidelines:

The motive is love.

Before confronting someone, it is always a good idea to start with a prayer. Check your motive. Why are you confronting? Are you angry? Do you enjoy pointing out someone else's mistakes? Is this the right time and place? Is the other person in the right frame of mind to respond to the confrontation? You may one day need to be confronted yourself, so it's wise to deal with others in the same way that you would like to be approached. Always start by stating a positive.

Example: A volunteer says to Mary, "I am pleased that you are doing so well in your computer course. But it seems you are having a problem with budgeting. May I discuss this with you?"

Change cannot be forced.

It's natural to want people to see your point of view and change their behavior accordingly. But you can't force people to change. So don't set changing another person as your goal. Speak clearly, listen with an open mind, and leave the responsibility for choices and change to the other person.

Example: Don't say, "Well, Mary, you will just have to learn to follow a budget." Say, "Mary, let's discuss your budget situation and see if we can come up with some better solutions."

Talk about behavior, don't attack the person.

Remember: A person and the person's behavior are two different things. Use specific examples and focus on the behavior. Eliminate words like *never* or *always*. *Example:* Don't say, "Mary, you're always out of money. Here it is the third week of the month and you've spent your entire monthly income already." Say, "Mary, during the past three months, you have not had any money available for the last week of the month."

Be a good listener.

Don't assume that you have all the facts and all the answers. Listen to the other person without interrupting. Restate what you are hearing and then ask if they want to add anything else.
Example: Don't say, "I'm not interested in excuses." Say, "Tell me why you think this is happening, Mary."

Don't be put off by a negative response.

It's natural to be defensive when confronted. The person may offer excuses, blame others, become angry, or verbally attack you. If the other person expresses these feelings, do not judge him or her. Just bring the discussion back to the issue at hand. *Example:* Mary explodes, "I *hate* cooking and you are always bugging me to cook meals to save money. So when I can't take it any more, I end up buying junk food for a week and then I don't have any money left for anything else."

You respond, "I understand. There are times when I don't feel like cooking either. Let's see what we can come up with to address the cooking issues and still live within your budget."

Identify a solution that is acceptable to everyone.

If you have followed all of the guidelines, it's quite likely that the person being confronted will now be willing to make some changes. Try to arrive at a solution that incorporates the person's desires while moving to resolve the issue that caused the confrontation.
Example: You say, "How about having a junk food night once a week when you know you won't have to cook? I just bought a 10-minute recipe book, and perhaps we could look at it together and choose some recipes that will work better for you on the nights when you have to cook. Would you like to try that?" Mary nods in agreement, and this confrontation has been successful.

Don't be discouraged if people don't change right away. It takes time to break bad habits and learn to implement brand new ones.

Notes

Notes

Notes

Notes

About Family Research Council

Founded in 1983, the Family Research Council is a nonprofit research and educational organization dedicated to articulating and advancing a family-centered philosophy of public life. In addition to providing policy research and analysis for the legislative, executive, and judicial branches of the federal government, the Council seeks to inform the news media, the academic community, business leaders, and the general public about family issues that affect the nation. Among its efforts to educate citizens for responsible engagement in public life is the Witherspoon Fellowship, a civic and cultural leadership program for college students.

The Family Research Council relies solely on the generosity of individuals, families, foundations, and businesses for financial support. The Internal Revenue Service recognizes the Council as a tax-exempt, 501(c)(3) charitable organization. Donations to the Council are therefore tax-deductible in accordance with section 170 of the Internal Revenue Code.

Located at 801 G Street, N.W., Washington, D.C., the headquarters of the Family Research Council provides its staff with strategic access to government decision-making centers, national media offices, and information sources. Owned by Faith Family Freedom, L.L.C., the six-story office building was completed in 1996 through the generosity of the Edgar Prince and Richard DeVos families of western Michigan. Visitors are welcome during normal business hours. Please call (202)393-2100 in advance to ensure a pleasant and productive visit.

FAMILY RESEARCH COUNCIL
801 G Street, N.W.
Washington, DC 20001
1-800-225-4008
www.frc.org